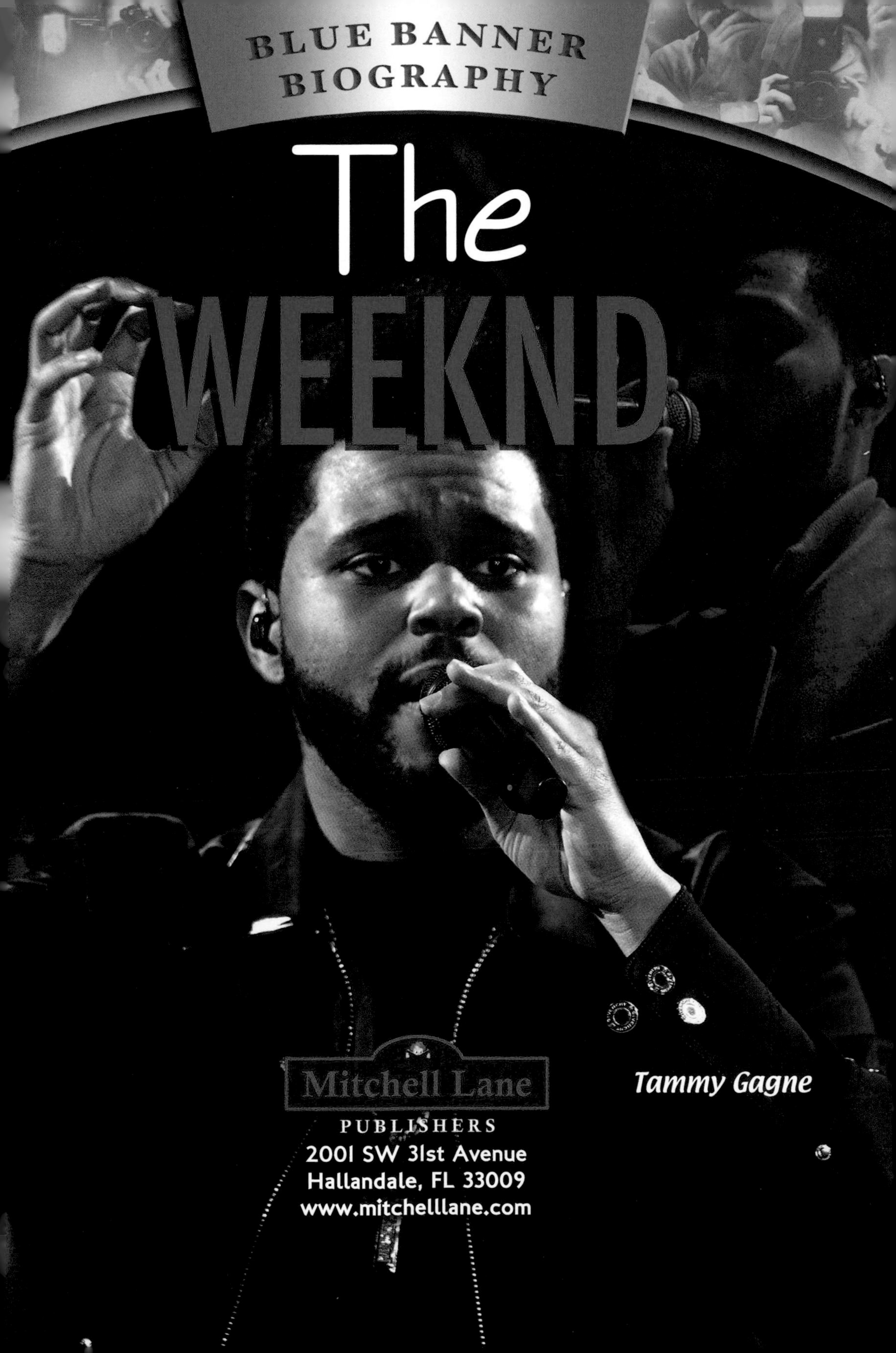

BLUE BANNER
BIOGRAPHY

# The
# WEEKND

Mitchell Lane
PUBLISHERS

2001 SW 31st Avenue
Hallandale, FL 33009
www.mitchelllane.com

*Tammy Gagne*

Printing   1      2      3      4      5      6      7      8      9

**Blue Banner Biographies**

**Library of Congress Cataloging-in-Publication Data**
Names: Gagne, Tammy.
Title: The Weeknd / by Tammy Gagne.
Description: Hallandale, FL : Mitchell Lane Publishers, [2018] | Series: Blue banner biographies | Includes bibliographical references and index.
Identifiers: LCCN 2017024476 | ISBN 9781680201246 (library bound)
Subjects: LCSH: Weeknd, 1990– —Juvenile literature. | Singers—Canada—Biography—Juvenile literature.
Classification: LCC ML3930.W406 G34 2018 | DDC 782.42164092 [B] —dc23
LC record available at https://lccn.loc.gov/2017024476

eBook ISBN: 978-1-68020-125-3

**ABOUT THE AUTHOR:** Tammy Gagne is the author of numerous books for adults and children, including *Ed Sheeran* and *Derek Hough* for Mitchell Lane Publishers. She resides in northern New England with her husband and son. One of her favorite pastimes is visiting schools to speak to kids about the writing process.

# Blue Banner Biography

*The Weeknd's many fans would know his face anywhere. But that wasn't always the case. Before he began performing in front of audiences, no one knew what the singer looked like. Not even record label executives knew anything beyond the fact that he was an incredibly talented singer.*

# CHAPTER 1

# *The Man Behind The Weeknd*

"**T**urn the music off, and come to dinner!" Jordan's father yelled. She had no idea he was making her favorite dish, baked macaroni and cheese. Her room was too far from the kitchen for the delicious scent to reach her. But he could hear the song she was playing like he was standing beside her. "Teenagers . . ." he muttered to himself as his daughter's approaching footsteps replaced the beat of the music.

As they began eating, Jordan's father told her that she reminded him of himself as a younger person. He grinned. "My mother constantly used to tell me to turn down my music. My favorite singer was Michael Jackson. The Weeknd actually sounds a lot like him."

"You *know* who The Weeknd is?" Jordan asked. She was surprised that her father was familiar with the artist she had been listening to while doing her homework.

"Of course I do," he responded. "I don't live under a rock." He had often heard the song "Can't Feel My Face" on the radio. He even found himself dancing to it while preparing their dinner that evening. It was an incredibly catchy tune.

"He sounds even more like Michael on 'I Feel it Coming,'" she said.

It was her father's turn to act surprised. "You mean, you know who Michael Jackson is?" He was teasing her. He had played Jackson's music in the house since Jordan was a baby. "You will have to play that song for me later."

> **People often think The Weeknd is an incredibly serious person. While some of his music is upbeat, many of his biggest hits are sad.**

"Did you hear that The Weeknd is playing a concert at the Verizon Center in a couple of months?" she asked. Her father had been expecting the subject of a concert to come up soon. She was getting older, after all.

"I had not heard that," he confessed. "Let me guess. You were wondering if I will let you go with your friends?" They would have to discuss it. But he remembered how thrilled he was to hear his own music idol in person for the first time. He had been just about Jordan's age.

"Actually, I was thinking maybe we could go together." She quickly added with a smile, "You know, just so you can hear the rest of his songs."

*****

The Weeknd's rise to fame began in 2011. Since that time he has become one of the biggest and most unique artists in the world. Today he can rarely go anywhere without being recognized. But that wasn't always the case.

Abel Tesfaye, the man who performs as The Weeknd, didn't even want his face or real name revealed in the beginning.

"I'm overwhelmed and grateful for my success. I also controlled how famous I was getting," he told Lisa Robinson of *Vanity Fair*. "I slowly would reveal more of myself every year. That helped me cope with fame as opposed to it all just falling on me."

He thought that not attaching his face to his music made it more mysterious. He also wasn't comfortable with the way he looked on camera. Even some of the biggest celebrities can feel unsure about their appearance. In his case, though, his **insecurity** became an advantage. Not even his most devoted fans had any idea of what he looked like until he began performing in public.

People often think The Weeknd is an incredibly serious person. While some of his music is upbeat, many of his biggest hits are sad. As a child, he listened to his mother's Ethiopian music. Although the songs were about heartbreak, he could not make out the lyrics. Still, he sensed their meaning. He thinks this inspired some of his gloomier songs.

The sadness doesn't stay with him. "People always say when they meet me that I'm not what they expect," he explained to Robinson. "I assume they think I'm this super dark and depressing guy, but I like to channel all of those emotions into my work. I'm pretty laid-back in real life. I just love hanging with my friends and making jokes."

*Abel Tesfaye is the man behind the face and voice of the now-famous musician The Weeknd. He is seen here performing at the 2012 OVO Fest at the Molson Canadian Amphitheatre, located in Toronto. The annual multi-act concert is sponsored by OVO Sound, the record label of superstar rapper and producer Drake.*

# Abel's Early Years

Abel Makkonen Tesfaye was born on February 16, 1990 in Scarborough, a neighborhood in the east side of Toronto, Canada. His parents, Makkonen and Samra Tesfaye, migrated to Canada from Ethiopia in the late 1980s. The couple split up shortly after Abel's birth. His mother raised him with the help of his grandmother. He grew up hearing them both speak Amharic, Ethiopia's native language. His fans can hear a bit of Amharic at the end of his song, "The Hills."

Ethiopian culture was an important part of Abel's childhood. He often attended an Ethiopian Orthodox church with his grandmother while his mother worked. He listened to Ethiopian singers, such as Aster Aweke. These performers **influenced** his now-famous vocal style. And he ate Ethiopian food, which he still loves even though he describes it as fattening.

Abel has maintained a strong bond with his mother throughout his life. He doesn't hesitate to give her credit for the person he has become and says that everything good about him came directly from her. Still, he was lonely as a child with no siblings. He especially wanted a brother to play with. He even told people that he had brothers. Though it was a lie, it reflected how badly he wanted at least one.

On the other hand, Abel has had little contact with his father, who played almost no part in Abel's upbringing. He remembers very little about him.

> Despite all the challenges Abel faced and the bad decisions he made, he held onto a deep appreciation for music. To this day he cares more about writing quality music than having a hit.

Abel didn't get the best grades in school. One reason might have been that he began taking drugs while he was still in middle school. For a while he was in a French **immersion** class. This meant that he had to speak French all day long. He hated it. Around this time his mother signed him up for piano lessons. He liked the instrument. But he preferred pop and rap music to classical.

He decided to drop out of high school when he was 17 to pursue a career in music. He left home one weekend with his friend Lamar Taylor. At that time he did not like his given name. The timing of their departure—during the weekend—led to Abel's stage name because it was such an important turning point in his life. But another Canadian band called The Weekend already existed. It had been formed in 1998 in London, a city a little over 100 miles from Toronto. Abel simply dropped the third "e" to avoid legal problems.

He remembers in great detail the day he left home, especially the sad way his mother looked at him. It seemed to him that she believed she had failed as a parent. Once his career took off, Abel wanted to do something nice for her. He bought a large house in Toronto for her. Though sometimes he thinks that she still wants him to get his high school diploma.

It took Abel a while to start working seriously on his music. When he moved out on his own, he was still taking drugs. He has said if he wasn't high at this time, he wasn't happy. After being **evicted** from his first apartment, Abel got a job at an American Apparel clothing store. And he began writing and recording his own songs.

Lamar uploaded Abel's first three songs, "The Morning," "What You Need," and "Loft Music," to YouTube in 2010. He didn't include Abel's name or any photos of him, just the music itself. The two young men asked friends to post links to the songs on Facebook. Soon other people began sharing the links on their own social media pages. Abel recalls going to work and hearing his coworkers play his music without even realizing it was him singing.

Despite all the challenges Abel faced and the bad decisions he made, he held onto a deep appreciation for music. To this day he cares more about writing quality music than having a hit. "The production can be cool and crazy-sounding," he explained to Radio.com, "but that's just special effects. If you can't strip it down and play it on piano, it's not a good song."

The Weeknd appeared on stage at the American Music Awards in November, 2014. He joined Ariana Grande to perform their duet "Love Me Harder" at the popular awards show in Los Angeles.

# CHAPTER 3

# *It All Began with a Mixtape*

**A**bel kept recording and sharing his music. He also continued hiding his face and real name. Doing so proved to be a smart strategy. In 2011, he recorded a mixtape called *House of Balloons* under his stage name, The Weeknd. Sometimes called "street albums," mixtapes are basically albums produced for **exposure** instead of sales. The Weeknd released *House of Balloons* for free on his website. It included 10 songs: his first three that had played on YouTube and seven new ones. The talented young singer started attracting attention of some powerful people in the recording business.

People everywhere were wondering about The Weeknd. Was it a person or a group? Some people suspected The Weeknd was a fake name for an artist who was already well known. No matter what people thought about the secretive musician—or musicians—behind the *House of Balloons* mixtape, one thing was obvious. They loved the songs.

One of those people was Nate Albert, senior vice president of Republic Records. He said he was "freaked out" when he heard The Weeknd's voice for the first time and flew to Canada almost immediately. He was determined to sign the mysterious artist to his label.

When Zena Golden of *The Fader* asked Albert how he found the anonymous artist, he laughed. "I forget how I figured out how to get to him, but we have our ways of finding people. He was secretive, but they were open and they were meeting labels—I certainly wasn't the only person flying to Canada, people were really excited about him."

At first The Weeknd didn't seem interested in any of the offers he was receiving. But Albert didn't give up. He pursued The Weekend for a year and a half. Finally, The Weeknd agreed to sign with him and his company. His first album with Republic Records, *Kiss Land*, came out in 2013.

*Kiss Land* was not the big success that The Weeknd and Albert had hoped it would be. The Weeknd seemed to have a small but steady fan base. But he wasn't winning over everyday people who listened to pop music. At first this setback devastated him. He even fell into a creative rut. He wrote enough songs to fill another album and half of a third but ended up tossing them away.

> *Regardless of how people wanted to classify him, The Weeknd used his fear to drive himself forward. He didn't want to be someone who could have been great but somehow fell short.*

He began listening to the music from other artists on his new label. Through this process, he learned more and more about pop music. The Weeknd is often called an R&B (rhythm and blues) artist. But he rejects this classification.

He thinks the only thing that might put him in the R&B category is his style of singing. "My inspiration is R. Kelly, Michael Jackson, and Prince, for the vocals anyway. My production and songwriting, and the environment around those vocals are not inspired by R&B at all," he explained to Claire Lobenfeld of Stereogum.com.

In particular, The Weeknd is frank about the influence Michael Jackson has had on his career. "Michael, man, that guy was the star,' he told Derrick Kennedy of the *Los Angeles Times*. "He invented the star. There will never be another Michael. I want to make it very clear that I'm not trying to be Michael. He's everything to me, so you're going to hear it in my music."

Regardless of how people wanted to classify him, The Weeknd used his fear to drive himself forward. He didn't want to be someone who could have been great but somehow fell short. He wanted to be big. He wanted to be a star.

When Republic Records suggested that The Weeknd record a duet with Ariana Grande for her 2014 album *My Everything*, he wasn't sure about the idea. He liked her song "Love Me Harder." But he couldn't picture himself singing it. He wanted to rewrite the lyrics to make the song a bit darker. The producer approved his changes. Pop music fans loved the end result. The song spent 22 weeks on the Billboard music chart. It made it all the way to number 7. It was his first top-10 single. The Weeknd was finally getting a **mainstream** audience.

By the time The Weeknd appeared at the 2015 iHeartRadio Musical Festival in Las Vegas, he had become one of the biggest musical artists. Today he has a huge fan base, which is made up of a wide variety of listeners.

## CHAPTER 4

# *Crossing Boundaries*

The Weeknd's second album, *Beauty Behind the Madness*, helped make 2015 a spectacular year for this rising star. It would eventually sell more than four million copies. By the middle of the summer, his hit single from the album, "Can't Feel My Face," had made it all the way to the top spot on the Billboard chart. During a concert in New York's Central Park, music legend Stevie Wonder sang a few bars of the song.

The Weeknd also performed the popular tune himself on stage in New Jersey with Taylor Swift. She invited him to appear as a surprise guest during her show. But the surprise was his when the crowd went wild. The Weeknd was stunned. He had no idea that he would get such an enthusiastic reception.

This event hinted at even more success for The Weeknd. As Sharon Dastur, senior vice president of programming at iHeartRadio, told Simon Vozick-Levenson of *Rolling Stone*, "He's absolutely one of the biggest artists out right now, and he's just getting going. Not a lot of

# SOUL

Just one year after performing at the 2014 American Music Awards, The Weeknd returned to the stage. This time it was to accept one of the awards. He was named Favorite Soul/R&B Male Artist at the event.

# /R&B

# MALE

The Weeknd is seen here at the Republic Records Holiday Party in New York City in 2015. Republic executives Charlie Walk, Avery Lipman, and Monte Lipman joined The Weeknd in celebrating his banner year at the event.

artists hit Number One this quickly and **navigate** all those formats."

The Weeknd echoed Dastur. "I feel like I'm changing pop culture," he told Vozick-Levenson. "Taylor Swift's audience can listen to me, but so can the street kids. I want to touch it all."

As *Beauty Behind the Madness* continued to produce hits, The Weeknd was appearing live more and more. He headlined the Billboard Hot 100 Festival and performed at the MTV Video Music Awards. He even appeared in television commercials for Apple Music. The musician who landed his big break by hiding his face and name was now a highly visible pop star.

He was also earning **recognition** for his work. In December, *Beauty Behind the Madness* received seven Grammy nominations. These included Record of the Year and Album of the Year.

Before the awards ceremony, The Weeknd took a month off to go home to Toronto. He spent about a week of this long vacation sleeping. He also went several periods without speaking to help rest his overworked voice.

The Weeknd faced intense competition at the Grammy awards, which were held February 15, 2016, in Los Angeles. He was up against Taylor Swift, Ed Sheeran, and Bruno Mars for Record of the Year. Although Mars snagged that honor, The Weeknd took home his first two Grammys. He won Best R&B Performance for his song "Earned It" and Best Urban Contemporary Album for *Beauty Behind the Madness*.

He also earned a standing **ovation** for his performance of "In the Night." Certainly he must have been getting used to this kind of reaction from crowds. But there was one big difference between his typical crowds and the audience at the Staples Center that night. This audience

The Weeknd happily poses with his two Grammys after the show.

*The Weeknd performs his song "Earned It" at the Academy Awards in February, 2016. Dancers, gymnasts, musicians, and trapeze artists help him recreate the energy and excitement of the music.*

was filled with other musicians— his peers. And they loved him as much as his many other fans did.

The Weeknd wasn't through with awards shows. "Earned It" was nominated for the Academy Award for Best Song. It was the lead single of the soundtrack to the movie *Fifty Shades of Grey*. Two weeks after the Grammys, The Weekend performed "Earned It" during the Oscar ceremony. While it didn't win, many people thought that the presentation—which included a dazzling array of dancers, gymnasts, and trapeze artists—was the highlight of the evening.

The Weeknd closed out his eventful year by releasing *Starboy*, his third album, in November. It debuted at number one on the Billboard 200.

*The Weeknd closed out his eventful year by releasing Starboy, his third album, in November. It debuted at number one on the Billboard 200.*

*The Weeknd met up with music legend Stevie Wonder at the Republic Records Grammy after-party in 2017.*

# Giving Back and Moving Forward

Shortly before *Starboy* was released, The Weeknd made a major life change. If there was one thing he had become known for as much as his music, it was his hair. Many celebrities are constantly changing their looks. But The Weeknd did not feel the need to do that. Instead, he just kept growing his dreadlocks longer and longer. "This is my natural hair, it's growing naturally, and I love it," he told Lisa Robinson of *Vanity Fair* in December, 2015. "It gives me an identity—I feel like it gives me powers sometimes. I came really close to cutting it once, but then I realized that I would just look like everyone else. That would be boring."

But eventually everyone needs a change. He finally decided to cut his hair about a year later. He had grown tired of the spiky dreadlocks interfering with his sleep. He could only sleep on one side of his face. There was another benefit. He didn't have to spend as much time cleaning his shower.

There was a third benefit as well. He didn't especially enjoy being chased by the **paparazzi**. His new 'do made him less visible. "If I had a great car, with my old hair, it was hard," he explained to Sasha Frere-Jones of *Billboard*. "Now? It's a breeze. I just put the hat on. My life is one hundred times better. I respect the paparazzi, it's their job, I got no beef with them. Luckily, for me, my career is putting out the hits and interacting with the fans. I don't need pictures of me being generated all the time."

> *The Weeknd focuses on the joy he receives from his work. He even enjoys the spotlight now.*

With the increasing popularity of his work, The Weeknd has inspired many other recording artists. Just as one can hear the sounds of Michael Jackson and Prince in The Weeknd's music, fans notice other artists sounding like him. He isn't bothered by this. "It means what we're doing is connecting with people," he told Garrick Kennedy of the *Los Angeles Times*. "I mean you don't want people to listen to your music and go, 'I don't want to do this.' But only I can do what I do. It doesn't feel like a threat or anything, it's flattering. I would actually love to **collaborate** with a lot of the young artists coming out."

One of the best parts of becoming a successful musician is being able to make a difference for important causes. When a celebrity speaks publicly about an issue, it is bound to get more attention. Many people look up to famous artists such as musicians and often listen to what they say with an open mind.

In The Weeknd's case, one of the causes he cares about the most is the Black Lives Matter movement. This national organization was created in 2012. It works to maintain the rights and dignity of black people throughout the United States. In July 2016, The Weeknd tweeted in support of Black Lives Matter. "Enough is enough," he declared. "It's time to stand up for this. We can either sit and watch, or do something about it. The time is now."

The Weeknd never intended to become an **activist**. "I promised myself that I would never tweet or talk about politics and focus on the music," he explained to Camilla Augustin of *Vibe*, "but I was just so bewildered that we lost more of our people to these senseless police shootings. It's hard to wrap my head around the fact that there are people who can't or won't see what Black Lives Matter is trying to accomplish." He did more than simply offer his words. He also donated $250,000 to the cause.

He cares a great deal about his culture and community. Although The Weeknd still hasn't finished his own education, he donated $50,000 to the University of Toronto in 2014 for its Ethiopian studies course. He also gave $50,000 to St. Mary Ethiopian Orthodox Church in Toronto in 2016.

His life has changed so much since those early years in Toronto. The music on *Starboy* is vastly different from the songs his friend posted to YouTube. From the beginning, it seems, The Weeknd has done things his own way. Perhaps that is one of the things that gives his music its unique sound. He sees his music as a way of recording his own experiences. "The vibe just represents how I feel," he told Garrick Kennedy, "what relationship I'm going through, what friendships I'm going through, the success in my life, the failures in my life. It is all just documentation."

The Weeknd focuses on the joy he receives from his work. He even enjoys the spotlight now. He especially relishes the feeling of going out on stage and knowing that many people in the audience are singing along with him. His "documentation" becomes theirs as well.

## CHRONOLOGY

| | |
|---|---|
| **1990** | Abel Makkonen Tesfaye is born in Toronto, Canada. |
| **2007** | He drops out of high school and moves away from home to pursue a music career. |
| **2010** | Abel's friend Lamar Taylor uploads three of his songs to YouTube. |
| **2011** | He releases the mixtape *House of Balloons*. |
| **2013** | He releases *Kiss Land*, his first album with Republic Records. |
| **2014** | The Weeknd releases the duet "Love Me Harder" with Ariana Grande. He donates $50,000 to the University of Toronto. |
| **2015** | He releases his second album, *Beauty Behind the Madness*. Taylor Swift invites The Weeknd to perform on stage during her concert in New Jersey. He performs at the MTV Video Music Awards. |
| **2016** | The Weeknd wins two Grammy awards. He releases his third album, *Starboy*. He donates $250,000 to Black Lives Matter and $50,000 to St. Mary Ethiopian Orthodox Church in Toronto. |
| **2017** | The Weeknd begins his Starboy: Legend of the Fall tour. |

## AWARDS

| | |
|---|---|
| **2015** | American Music Award, Favorite Soul/R&B Album for *Beauty Behind the Madness* |
| **2016** | Billboard Music Award, Top Hot 100 Artist |
| | Billboard Music Award, Top R&B Album for *Beauty Behind the Madness* |
| | Billboard Music Award, Top R&B Song for "The Hills" |
| | Billboard Music Award, Top Radio Songs Artist |
| | Billboard Music Award, Top Song Sales Artist |
| | Billboard Music Award, Top Streaming Song for "The Hills" |
| | Grammy, Best R&B Performance for "Earned It" |
| | Grammy, Best Urban Contemporary Album for *Beauty Behind the Madness* |
| | People's Choice Award, Favorite R&B Artist |

## DISCOGRAPHY

**2011**  *House of Balloons*
          *Thursday*
          *Echoes of Silence*
**2012**  *Trilogy*
**2013**  *Kiss Land*
**2015**  *Beauty Behind the Madness*
**2016**  *Starboy*

## GLOSSARY

**activist** (AK-tuh-vist) — a person who stands up and speaks out for a cause

**collaborate** (kuh-LAB-uh-rayt) — to work together with another person or group on a common project

**evict** (ee-VIKT) — to order a tenant to move out of a property

**exposure** (ek-SPOH-zher) — presentation for public viewing and enjoyment

**immersion** (ih-MUR-zhuhn) — the act of concentrating on a subject for an extended period of time to learn about it as quickly as possible

**influence** (in-FLOO-uhnss) — to affect or move to action

**insecurity** (in-sih-KYOOR-uh-tee) — a lack of self-confidence

**mainstream** (MANE-streem) — belonging to a widely accepted group

**navigate** (NAV-ih-gayt) — to move through a process in a logical sequence

**ovation** (oh-VAY-shuhn) — energetic applause

**paparazzi** (pah-puh-RAHT-zee) — freelance photographers who take and sell candid pictures of celebrities

**recognition** (rek-ugh-NISH-uhn) — acknowledgement of the merit of a person or work

**PHOTO CREDITS:** Cover, p. 1 (front) — Pascal Le Segretain/Staff/Getty Images for Victoria's Secret, (background) — Christopher Polk/Staff/Getty Images for Interscope Records; p. 4 — Kyle Gustafson/ZUMA Wire/Alamy Live News/ZUMA Press, Inc./Alamy Stock Photo; p. 8 — DCP/N8N photo/Alamy Stock Photo; pp. 12, 18-19, 22 — Kevin Winter/Staff/Getty Images Entertainment; p. 16 — David Becker/Stringer/Getty Images for iHeartMedia; p. 19 — Dimitrios Kambouris/Staff/Getty Images Entertainment; p. 21 — Frederick M. Brown/Stringer/Getty Images Entertainment; p. 24 — Rachel Murray/Stringer/Getty Images for Republic Records.

## FURTHER READING

### Books

Bilo, Berne. *The Weeknd: Flying High to Success, Weird and Interesting Facts on Abel Tesfaye*. Charleston, SC: CreateSpace, 2017.
Braun, Eric. *Prince: The Man, the Symbol, the Music*. Minneapolis: Lerner, 2017.
Stine, Megan. *Who Was Michael Jackson?* New York: Grossett and Dunlap, 2015.

### On the Internet

Billboard, The Weeknd
    http://www.billboard.com/artist/419413/weeknd
The Weeknd
    https://www.theweeknd.com/
The Weeknd—Facebook
    https://www.facebook.com/theweeknd/

### Works Consulted

Caramanica, Jon. "Can The Weeknd Turn Himself Into the Biggest Pop Star in the World?" *The New York Times Magazine*, July 27, 2015. https://www.nytimes.com/2015/08/02/magazine/can-the-weeknd-turn-himself-into-the-biggest-pop-star-in-the-world.html?_r=3
Caulfield, Keith. "The Weeknd's 'Beauty Behind the Madness' Debuts at No. 1 on Billboard 200 Chart." *Billboard*, September 6, 2015. http://www.billboard.com/articles/columns/chart-beat/6685947/the-weeknd-beauty-behind-the-madness-debuts-at-no-1-billboard-200-charts
Eells, Josh, "Sex, Drugs and R&B: Inside The Weeknd's Dark Twisted Fantasy." *Rolling Stone*, October 21, 2015. http://www.rollingstone.com/music/features/sex-drugs-and-r-b-inside-the-weeknds-dark-twisted-fantasy-20151021
Frere-Jones, Sasha. "The Weeknd Opens Up About Paparazzi and Overcoming Stage Fright in Rare Interview." *Billboard*, December 12, 2016. http://www.billboard.com/articles/events/year-in-music-2016/7616356/the-weeknd-interview-starboy-no-1s
Giorgis, Hannah. "The Weeknd's East African Roots." *Pitchfork*, June 11, 2015. http://pitchfork.com/thepitch/793-the-weeknds-east-african-roots/
Golden, Zara. "The Weeknd's A&R On His Transformation From Icy Internet Star To Pop Maven." *Fader*, August 26, 2015. http://www.thefader.com/2015/08/26/the-weeknds-ar-on-his-transformation-from-icy-internet-star-to-pop-star-and-ibeauty-behind-the-madnessi

FURTHER READING

Kennedy, Gerrick D. "How The Weeknd got his revenge and became one of the biggest pop stars." *Los Angeles Times*, February 12, 2016. http://www.latimes.com/entertainment/music/la-ca-ms-weeknd-grammys-conversation-20160211-htmlstory.html

Ledbetter, Carly. "9 Things You Need to Know About The Weeknd." *The Huffington Post*, February 11, 2016. http://www.huffingtonpost.com/entry/the-weeknd-trivia_us_56bb63cfe4b08ffac1236c5e

Levine, Nick. "Ready for The Weeknd: What Makes the Enigmatic R&B Star Tick." NME, November 17, 2016. http://www.nme.com/features/what-the-weeknd-is-made-of-1860541

Lobenfeld, Claire. "Read The Weeknd's First-Ever Interview." Stereogum, July 15, 2013. http://www.stereogum.com/1406832/read-the-weeknds-first-ever-interview/news/

Merritt, Jason. "Kendrick Lamar, Taylor Swift, The Weeknd win early Grammys." CBS News, February 15, 2016. http://www.cbsnews.com/news/kendrick-lamar-taylor-swift-the-weeknd-win-early-grammys/

Min, Lilian. "The Weeknd donated $50,000 to a cause dear to his heart." Hello Giggles, August 7, 2016. http://hellogiggles.com/weeknd-donated-50000-cause-dear-heart/

Robinson, Lisa. "The Weeknd Gets His Power from an Unexpected Source." *Vanity Fair*, December 2015. http://www.vanityfair.com/culture/2015/11/the-weeknd-on-bella-hadid-fame

Ruffo, Jillian. "Here's the Real Reason The Weeknd Cut Off His Famous Dreadlocks." *People*, November 4, 2016. http://people.com/style/the-weeknd-explains-short-haircut/

Takeda, Allison. "The Weeknd Earns a Standing Ovation for Soulful Grammys 2016 Performance." *Us Magazine*, February 15, 2016. http://www.usmagazine.com/entertainment/news/the-weeknd-gets-a-standing-ovation-for-grammys-2016-performance-w164438

Vozick-Levenson, Simon. "How The Weeknd Went From Broke in Canada to Sharing Stage with Taylor Swift." *Rolling Stone*, August 21, 2015. http://www.rollingstone.com/music/features/how-the-weeknd-went-from-broke-in-canada-to-sharing-stage-with-taylor-swift-20150821

Wicks, Amanda. "The Weeknd on Ariana Grande and the Art of Pop Music." Radio.com, October 21, 2015. http://radio.com/2015/10/21/the-weeknd-on-ariana-grande-and-the-art-of-pop-music/

Wilson, Carl. "Billboard Cover: The Weeknd on Why 'Nobody Can Stop Me But Myself.'" *Billboard*, August 27, 2015. http://www.billboard.com/articles/news/magazine-feature/6677740/the-weeknd-beauty-behind-the-madness-album-taylor-swift-max-martin-michael-jackson

# INDEX